silence

Hoa Pham

Currency Press,
Sydney

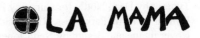

CURRENCY PLAYS

First published in 2010
by Currency Press Pty. Ltd.,
PO Box 2287, Strawberry Hills, NSW, 2012, Australia.
enquiries@currency.com.au
www.currency.com.au
in association with
La Mama Theatre, Melbourne

Copyright © Hao Pham 2009, 2010.

COPYING FOR EDUCATIONAL PURPOSES
The Australian *Copyright Act 1968* (Act) allows a maximum of one chapter
or 10% of this book, whichever is the greater, to be copied by any educational
institution for its educational purposes provided that that educational institution
(or the body that administers it) has given a remuneration notice to Copyright
Agency Limited (CAL) under the Act.

For details of the CAL licence for educational institutions contact CAL,
19/157 Liverpool Street, Sydney, NSW, 2000. Tel: (02) 9394 7600;
Fax: (02) 9394 7601; E-mail: info@copyright.com.au

COPYING FOR OTHER PURPOSES
Except as permitted under the Act, for example a fair dealing for the purposes
of study, research, criticism or review, no part of this book may be reproduced,
stored in a retrieval system, or transmitted in any form or by any means without
prior written permission. All enquiries should be made to the publisher at the
address above.

Any performance or public reading of *Silence* is forbidden unless a licence has
been received from the author or the author's agent. The purchase of this book
in no way gives the purchaser the right to perform the play in public, whether
by means of a staged production or a reading. All applications for public
performance should be addressed c/- Currency Press.

NATIONAL LIBRARY OF AUSTRALIA CIP DATA

Author:	Pham, Hoa.
Title:	Silence / Hoa Pham.
ISBN:	9780868198781 (pbk.)
Series:	Current theatre series.
Subject:	Australian drama.
	Vietnamese drama
Dewey Number:	A822.4

Typeset by Dean Nottle for Currency Press.
Printed by Hyde Park Press, Richmond, SA.
Cover image and design by Nedd Jones.

Contents

Theatre program at end of playtext

ACKNOWLEDGEMENTS

With thanks to Lam Pham for the Vietnamese translations.

Hoa Pham and Wolf Heidecker would like to thank La Mama and the Australian Vietnamese Women's Welfare Association for their support in a short developmental work-in-progress season at La Mama in 2008. They would also like to thank HaiHa Le, Diana Nguyen, Mong Diep, Melanie Beddie and director Gorkem Acarolgu.

Dedicated to my grandparents and Alister Air, who are always there for me.

Silence was first produced by La Mama at La Mama Courthouse, Carlton, on 11 November 2009, with the following cast:

BA	Hoa Pham
MA	Dianna Nguyen
DAO	Ai Diem Le
PUPPETEERS	Danielle Goronszy
	Paul Bongiorno

Dramaturgy, Kit Lazaroo
Director, Wolf Heidecker
Director of Puppetry, Penelope Bartlau
Sound Designer, Simon Charles
Puppet Maker, Danielle Goronszy
Movement Advisor, Paul Bongiorno

CHARACTERS

BA, grandmother
MA, mother, her daughter
DAO, granddaughter, about 18
HUNGRY GHOSTS

HUNGRY GHOSTS are spirits of the dead that have not gone to nirvana because no-one is praying for them, or they have died in violent ways and their issues are not yet resolved.

In production, the HUNGRY GHOSTS can be represented by puppetry.

In the notation of the play, the plural HUNGRY GHOSTS speak as a voice-over audio. The singular HUNGRY GHOST is a manifestation on stage.

SETTING

A couch and a kitchen table with chairs. An altar for the deceased with a picture of a man (the father of the family).

The prayers for the hungry ghosts recited in Scene One and Scene Five are from the Plum Village Chanting and Recitation book compiled by Thich Nhat Hanh and the monks and nuns of Plum Village.

SCENE ONE

BA *is moving freely in front of the stage. Her hair is down and she is dressed in white.*

Ghost music plays.

BA *stares into the audience.*

BA: You see what you see. I see what I see. Alone in this room I speak with the living and the dead.

> *A bell sounds.*

> *Audible whispering from* HUNGRY GHOSTS.

HUNGRY GHOSTS: [*in a mixture of Vietnamese and English, repeated*] *Cho ăn đi. Cúng đi. Làm quỉ đói đi.* [Feed us. Honour us. Become one of us.]

BA: Why did you abandon me, son? To your wife's care?

HUNGRY GHOSTS: You know, you know.

BA: What turned you bad? [*She scratches her rashes. She holds her head in her hands. Whispering*] I'm so ashamed. Of you. I'm so ashamed.

HUNGRY GHOSTS: Sacrifice. All you have sacrificed. You bear the family's shame. Join us. Come and join us.

BA: It would be so easy now to give up and go to sleep. Then no-one would need to look after me anymore.

> *Silence.*

> *A bell sounds.*

> DAO *and* MA*'s voices are heard praying.*

MA:
As if a fire is raging on all four sides,
A hungry ghost ceaselessly suffers from heat
Hungry ghost now to be born in a Pure Land
Hear this gatha transmitted by the Buddha

> *Bell.*

Hungry ghosts have acted unskillfully

DAO:
With craving, hatred and ignorance
Manifested in actions of body, speech and mind.
All hungry ghosts repent of this

Bell.

O hungry ghosts
DAO & MA: [*together*]
We make offerings of food
Multiplied in the ten directions
So that you can all receive them
By the merit of this offering
May we and all hungry ghosts
Be successful in the realisation of the path.

Bell.

BA *looks after them longingly then returns to the couch.*

Blackout.

Lights up, a bright day, cheerful.

Suddenly, DAO *is there, carrying a backpack and conical hat.*

BA: *Con đả về rồi!* [You've come home!]

DAO: *Chào Bà Nội. Bà có khỏe không?* [Greetings, grandmother. Are you in good health?]

BA: *Bà khỏe—Chỉ trừ mấy cái phong này. Ngủa quá.* [Except for these wretched rashes. They itch all the time.]

She rolls up her cardigan sleeves and scratches.

DAO: I have some presents for you.

BA: *Tụi Cộng sản có làm khó cho con không?* [The communists didn't give you a hard time?]

DAO: [*surprised*] Communists? No.

BA: *Bà con mình thì sao? Họ ghét người Việt Kiều như chúng mình lắm.* [What about our relatives? They hate us Viet Kieu.]

DAO: Not all Vietnamese hate the Viet Kieu. They like overseas Vietnamese. They bring money... And Auntie Chi was very grateful for what Mum gave her.

BA *pats a chair next to her and* DAO *sits down.*

BA: *Dì Chi ra sao? Dì có còn mở tiệm bán hàng không?* [So how is Auntie Chi? Does she still have her store?]

> DAO *digs out a present from her backpack.*

DAO: From Auntie Chi.

BA: *Ba không cần quà của Dì đâu.* [I don't need presents from them.] [*She opens the present. It's a pair of dainty slippers.*] *Làm sao mà bà đi giày này? Với chân bà như thế này?* [How am I supposed to wear these? With my feet?]

DAO: They'll fit you.

BA: These are for ladies of leisure like your Auntie Chi. I've had to work hard standing on my feet. Is she well?

DAO: Yes. There's five of them living in the shop now. They have two mopeds and a DVD player so I guess they're doing well.

BA: Did you find a boyfriend over there?

> DAO *laughs.*

DAO: No way. I got followed around by a couple of creeps but that's all.

BA: They were just being friendly. That's how your grandfather courted me, you know.

DAO: It's called stalking now, Ba.

BA: You have his eyes.

> *She takes her hand.*

Your skin is so beautiful and smooth. *Đẹp quá.* [*She notices the conical hat next to the backpack.*] I used to wear one of those. What did you bring old peasant garb back for?

> DAO *shrugs.*

When I was your age I was cycling fifty kilometres a day to sell goods.

DAO: Auntie Chi told me what you used to do.

> BA *starts scratching.*

BA: My rashes are really bothering me. Did you get some of Auntie Chi's ointment for me?

> DAO *sits back down next to* BA *and hands her the ointment.*

DAO: Smells of gum trees. Auntie Chi says it's the best stuff…

BA: Tiger balm oil.

DAO: Where's Mum?

BA: You've forgotten, haven't you?

DAO: Forgotten what?

BA: Your father's second death anniversary is tomorrow morning.

MA comes in overladen with groceries. DAO goes and helps her.

MA carefully puts oranges and apples on a plate offering to the shrine.

She barely glances at the photo on the shrine, for her this is just one more duty.

MA: I'm glad you're home.

DAO: I'm glad too. No-one cooks like you, Mum.

They embrace.

MA: Why didn't you tell me when you were arriving home? I would have picked you up from the airport...

DAO: Stacey came and picked me up, Mum.

MA: You never let me do anything for you. Always Stacey... You should ask family first.

Silence.

So how was Vietnam?

MA starts setting out the table for three.

Then BA fetches an extra plate leaving one empty plate at the head of the table. This would be the father's place if he was alive.

DAO: [*sarcarstically*] Is someone else coming for dinner?

BA: It's for your father's spirit.

DAO swears under her breath.

MA: So how was Vietnam?

DAO: The countryside was beautiful. Hanoi and Saigon were so crowded, the traffic was incredible...

MA: Did anyone bother you while you were there?

DAO looks at BA.

DAO: No. It was pretty safe. Kids were running around at nine at night.

BA: My rashes are really itchy. The cat keeps meowing, too.

DAO: Cat? What cat?

MA and BA ignore her.

DAO *gets* MA *a present from her backpack.*

MA *opens it. It's an* áo dài *(traditional Vietnamese dress).*

MA: That's beautiful. But where would I wear it?

DAO: Next time you go singing, Ma.

MA *scoffs.*

MA: I haven't sung for a long time. I've been too busy working.

DAO: You should go back to Vietnam for a holiday.

MA: Then who would look after Ba Noi? I have too many things to do here.

MA *serves dinner.*

The family sits down and begins to eat.

DAO: You cooked *buon bo*! You're the best, Mum!

MA: How was the food in Vietnam?

DAO: It was so fresh and cheap! Amazing! But the chicken was really bony, though.

MA: I remember looking after chickens when we lived in the South after fleeing from the North. We had to look after them and the ducks while my mother was at work in the city. It was the best time of my childhood.

BA: I heard that your neighbours were supposed to give you money so you could buy food. Instead you ate grass. Do you remember that? You can't trust anybody.

DAO: You ate grass?

MA: We tried it one day. We were really hungry. But these are all stories from the past. We are really lucky now.

MA *eats some food.*

BA: The cats are meowing again. I'm so weak. They took gallons of blood from me. Like when I sold my blood to three different hospitals to make money. If there's a war, Dao, I've hidden money under the couch. You remember it if we get in trouble.

DAO *stares at her.* MA *ignores her.*

MA: So how did you find Auntie Chi?

DAO: We got along really well. She told me heaps about the family when you were living back in Vietnam.

MA: Tomorrow is your father's death anniversary. I need your help to cook tomorrow morning.

DAO *takes in a breath.*

DAO: Mum, I've got other plans. I'm going out tonight with Stacey and I'm going to stay at her house...

MA: I need you here.

DAO: Ba can help...

MA: I need you, Dao. It's your duty.

BA: Have you fed her? She's hungry.

MA *and* BA *ignore her.*

DAO: We shouldn't be celebrating his death. He hasn't lived with us for years.

BA: Meow, meow.

DAO: [*gently*] There's no cat, Ba Noi.

MA: [*irritated*] She had cats back in Vietnam.

BA: I need to go to the toilet.

BA *exits stage.*

DAO: Is Ba losing it?

MA *looks at* DAO.

MA: She's been getting worse. She had a stroke when you were away.

DAO: A stroke? Why didn't you tell me?

MA: I didn't want to spoil your holiday. It was only a mild one. She was only in hospital for a few days.

DAO: You never tell me anything!

BA *returns.* DAO *looks earnestly at* BA.

Ba khoe khong?

BA: I get dizzy when I stand up.

DAO: I heard you were in hospital...

BA: My husband promised to visit me in hospital and he didn't. I had to borrow money to pay for the hospital when I was too weak to stand. I had to sneak out and get my clothes from the house. He never came with the clothes to the hospital that I told him to bring. Have we paid them yet?

MA: Yes we have.

DAO *looks at* MA *puzzled.*

She's remembering when your father was born.

DAO: Grandfather abandoned Ba Noi too, didn't he?

MA: Yes he did.

DAO: It runs in the family.

MA: You shouldn't say that, Dao.

DAO: Oh, stop trying to defend him all the time! Why did Dad leave us?

MA: Dao, enough.

DAO: Men only want one thing—

MA: Dao!

DAO: And we're better off without them!

MA: *Im*. Ssssh.

BA: The cats are meowing again. I had to leave them behind when we escaped on the fishing boat. I locked them in the house with bowls of rice so the neighbours would not know that we were gone for a few days. Meow, meow.

DAO: [*gently*] There are no cats, Ba Noi.

    BA *looks confused.*

MA: There's no point in trying to tell her that. Just ignore her.

DAO: You can't ignore everything.

MA: What are you saying? You're being really difficult today and you've just come home!

DAO: Auntie Chi opened up my eyes to a few things. She says us Viet Kieu are living in denial. You still think you can get your old life back by flying a few Southern flags. Whilst the Vietnamese have moved on. We lost and we're still clinging to the past.

MA: How can you say such a thing? You haven't suffered the way Ba Noi and I have suffered from the communists…

BA: Bloody communists. Under them, we had rations. One kilogram of meat a month per family.

MA: You really don't understand. You weren't on the boat journey, you didn't experience the conditions at the refugee camp in Malaysia— there was no food and we were starving…

    DAO *looks down at her food for a moment.*

BA: I was so relieved at first when we got to Malaysia on the mercy ship. Then we had such a long wait on the island. Ten thousand of us with hardly any food. I wondered if we had made a mistake. Then the white officials came and spoke to your father. We were chosen to go to Australia. We were so lucky.

MA: All the same, I expect you to stay home tonight, young lady, and help me prepare for tomorrow's ceremony.

DAO: I already told you, Mum. I've got plans…

BA: Stay home and help us cook. I can teach you how to cook.

DAO *sighs and nods her head at* BA*'s intervention.*

DAO: All right. I've got to call Stacey back.

She gets up from the table and produces her mobile phone. She exits the stage.

MA *finishes her dinner and takes* BA*'s plate.*

MA: She didn't even finish her dinner. With pork the price it is…

BA: My son was a good boy…

MA, *frustrated, snatches the plate from under* BA*'s nose, clears the table and stalks off stage.*

BA *is left sitting alone at the kitchen table.*

SCENE TWO

BA *is trying on her new slippers.*

MA *is trying on her new* áo dài.

DAO *is playing with the conical hat.*

DAO: I hate it here! Everyone is so fucking repressed! In Vietnam I had the best time, on mopeds with my cousins. One of them smokes dope and gambles—he lost six mobile phones. When his parents deny him anything he threatens to commit suicide. If I offed myself here no-one would notice.

MA *is humming to herself, the melody of a love song.*

When she sees the picture of her husband on the shrine she stops humming abruptly.

MA: It didn't used to be like this. I remember when you first took me out dancing.

A bell sounds.

HUNGRY GHOSTS: Remember us. Remember us. You see what you see. We see what we see.

BA: *Tụi quỉ này đến đây làm gì. Tao còn nhớ tụi bây.* [Why have you come? I remember you.]

> *She keeps speaking to them in Vietnamese. She sits.*

DAO: Now I know what Dad did to Mum… Auntie Chi told me so much. But how can I break it to Mum now? She's suffered so much…

MA: When you asked me to marry you, I thought I had shed my bad fortune. But then rumours started. At first I refuse to believe. My own sister would tell me you were bad and warned me. But I had to get away from my mother and father. They curse me as bad luck.

BA: I remember the shame of being in prison. No food. No family to come and visit. We would trade mouldy rice for a little bit of meat. We would plait our hair to make string for a washing line. One young girl was in prison for being a prostitute. She slept with a man who gave her a contagious disease. She did it for a bowl of *pho*.

HUNGRY GHOSTS: You remember, you remember.

> BA *shakes her head from side to side.*

BA: All these bad memories. I don't want to remember. My son went to war and he came back changed. They were all so young. We had to flee. He fought for the AR Vietnam. I remember going to work and seeing the corpses lying by the side of the road. Life is good now.

HUNGRY GHOSTS: Remember us. Remember us.

> *Silence.*

DAO: Why the hell are we still remembering you? You walked out on us leaving Ba behind. [*Pause.*] You disappearing was the best thing that ever happened to me… I'm glad you're dead and gone.

> *Pause.*

MA: At least you brought me to Australia. That's all I have to thank you for. I wanted to be a singer. You wouldn't let me go out. You said it was a waste of time. No-one would want to hear me sing. Now my duty is to look after your mother, so I am still bound to you.

> MA *keeps humming.*

BA: The Buddha says that to reach nirvana you have to find peace in yourself… I still have nightmares and see ghosts… There is no peace here…

HUNGRY GHOSTS: You have to honour us. Feed us. Acknowledge us. Honour us.

> BA *keeps speaking to the ghosts in Vietnamese.*

DAO: If only I didn't know… If only I could forget…

MA: I dream about being swept away. Off my feet under a starry moon… No-one knows. No-one can know. I am a respectable widow with a family to look after. Their happiness comes first.

> MA *hums.*

BA: The cats meow at night and make my rashes itch. In 1954 all the people were scared and ran away. I remember my first offerings. There was a funeral and I wasn't allowed to attend. The servants had to hold me back from joining the procession when it came by our house. We were rich then, my family owned land in the North. I remember being carried around in sedan chairs. [*She sits in a chair and peers forward as if being carried around in a sedan chair.*] I used to watch the peasants toil in the fields, ploughing the rice paddies with the water buffalo. I learnt French: 'Je parle français'. All the peasants loved my father. He was good to them and let them keep their surplus rice to sell. Now he is dead, dead from the war. [*She reaches for a bell.*] Every day I pray and honour the dead.

HUNGRY GHOSTS: Acknowledge us. Speak to us. Remember us, remember us.

> BA *rings the bell.*

SCENE THREE

The lounge room is dominated by the ancestral altar where there is a picture of a man flanked by candles and flowers.

DAO *is asleep on the couch, still in her nightclubbing clothes.*

MA *enters and clucks her tongue when she sees* DAO *still asleep.*

MA: Dao! Wake up!

> MA *shakes* DAO.

DAO: Wh… What?

MA: Wake up! You went out last night, didn't you? Serves you right. You have to help with the cooking.

DAO: What cooking?

MA: *Má đang làm gì đó?* [What are you doing?]

> DAO *comes back in.*

Dao, help your grandmother. [*Under her breath*] She's just making it worse.

> DAO *patiently helps* BA *sort out the greens.*
>
> *Silence.*

BA: Life is suffering. Identifying the root of suffering, then touching the root of suffering, one ceases to suffer.

> DAO *frowns.*

DAO: Mum, what is she talking about?

MA: [*irritable*] She's just reciting the four noble truths. Just ignore her.

> BA *stands up and walks over to the shrine, oblivious to how distressed she has made* DAO.

HUNGRY GHOSTS: Join us. Come and join us.

BA: I will come and join you soon. In my own time.

DAO: Who are you talking to, Ba Noi? [*Pause.*] There's nobody there...

> DAO *stares after her.*
>
> *The phone rings.*
>
> MA *picks it up.*

Hello... Oh, hello. [*Laughing*] No. I can't talk now... I can't please everybody!... Speak to you later.

> *She slams the phone down.*

Who was that?

> MA *ignores her.*
>
> MA *finishes preparing her dishes. She goes to the lounge room and puts a dish of food on the shrine.*

's time. We should pay our respects.

> *They get up from their chairs and go to the lounge to face the family altar where a photo of a young man is flanked by red and white flowers.*
>
> BA *reverently offers the altar a bowl of rice and lights incense.*
>
> *She hands incense to* MA *and* DAO.

MA *swears.*

MA: Your father's death anniversary is today. Get up. You're so la

DAO: I was out late last night…

MA: You've had enough sleep. Come on. Help me and Ba.

    Groaning, DAO *gets up.*

    DAO *joins* BA, *who is sorting greens in the kitchen.*

    MA *comes over and bosses* BA *around.*

Má để cái nào hư vào đây, còn cái nào tốt vào đây. [Put the
here, and the fresh ones there.]

    BA *nods.*

    DAO *yawns and sits down next to* BA.

DAO: Where's everyone else? Aren't the others coming to

    MA *ignores her and busies herself with pots and pa*

    DAO *looks to* BA.

Noi, why aren't the other aunties here to help?

BA: It's my favourite son's death anniversary. You are ver
out, Dao. [*To* MA] *Bé Đào ngoan quá?* [Isn't she goo

MA: Lazy, more like it. [*She looks at what* BA *is doing.*] I to
the stale ones from the fresh ones!

    BA *looks confused.*

BA: Back when I was young, when it was my great gran
sary all the aunties and uncles would come to help
We had suckling pork, duck's eggs and steamed f
feast even during the war time.

DAO: Yeah, well obviously no-one cares about Dad

    MA *ignores* DAO *again.*

BA: We have to have a feast for my favourite son's
will be a hungry ghost and hang around us. W
has to go to the other shore…

DAO: What are you talking about? He's gone. Ove
a party for the day he left…

BA: [*scratching the rashes on her arms*] We hon
them happy. The hungry ghosts… they are
peace to send them to nirvana…

BA *bows deeply three times to the altar.*

Then she plants the incense in the incense holder.

BA *lingers over the picture of her son.*

A bell sounds.

MA *bows to the photo shallowly three times then plants the incense.*

BA *looks at her disapprovingly.*

I've done my duty to your son.

BA: [*chiding*] Your husband.

DAO *bows abruptly once to the altar and shoves the incense in the holder.*

DAO: He's dead. Get over it.

MA: Dao! Don't be disrespectful! Otherwise you'll end up a hungry ghost wandering around with no-one to pay respects to you when you die…

HUNGRY GHOSTS: Like us, like us. Be one of us.

BA: Why do you hate him so much?

DAO *just stares at* BA *not knowing what to say.*

Why do you hate him so much? He is your father. You should not hate him.

Silence.

I will tell you a secret. Your mother cursed you with his mistress' name to make sure he knew she knew.

DAO *stares at* BA.

DAO: Is that true?

MA *says nothing.*

Is that true, Ba? Auntie Chi didn't tell me that…

HUNGRY GHOSTS: There is nothing left. Feed us. Feed us.

MA: Sit down, Dao. Have something to eat.

DAO *reluctantly sits down.* DAO, BA *and* MA *eat in silence.*

DAO: I am named after his mistress? I know about it, Mum. Auntie Chi told me. I didn't want to tell you, but… it explains everything…

MA: Explain what? Auntie Chi should have kept her mouth shut. I tried to protect you from that. You didn't need to know. What was she thinking?

DAO: You know.

MA: I don't know anything.

DAO: And how he treated me…

MA: What are talking about? You are lucky. Your father was not strict like some fathers. He never even smacked you. You have to be quiet about this around your grandmother, it just makes her worse…

DAO: You only care about what other people think! You don't really care about what really happens! You made me lie about Dad leaving for so long…

MA: It was necessary. Other people should not know of our pain…

DAO: I don't care what other people think!

> BA *looks up, confused at the tension between* MA *and* DAO.

BA: Why all this shouting?

> DAO *turns to* BA.

DAO: Did you know the truth about your son, Ba? Do you know why he left us?

BA: [*confused*] My son. He's dead now gone to the other shore…

DAO: Good riddance.

BA: Why are we so angry? We should be happy. Dao is back home now… Her father will be so happy to see his little girl….

> DAO *bursts into tears.*

> BA *peers at them genuinely puzzled. Then she turns her attention back to the shrine.*

My son. Where has he gone? [*She picks up the conical hat, lost in her memories of the past.*] The cats… they are crying again…

> *The* HUNGRY GHOST *approaches* BA *from behind.*

My only son. I left you behind in the orphanage.

HUNGRY GHOST: [*in a young boy's voice*] Má ơi, má ơi. Đừng bỏ con! Cho con đi theo! Đừng bỏ con một mình… [Ma, Ma! Don't leave me behind! Take me with you! Don't leave…]

> BA *begins to cry.*

BA: I couldn't afford to keep you. There was a war on, I had to earn money for food…

HUNGRY GHOST: [*an older male voice*] If you have seen what I have seen… During the war the men would hold drinking games. Six seconds. It would take six seconds before a grenade would blow up. We would put a grenade in a man's beer glass. Pull the pin. He would have to swallow it all in six seconds and throw the grenade away. If we were lucky everyone would be left standing at the end of the night.

BA: You came back changed. The war changed you. All the blood on your hands. You screamed in your sleep and I would tell you, it was all right, Mama is here, Mama is here…

HUNGRY GHOST: I could not bear to live with everything I had seen.

BA: [*shouting*] Then you abandoned me!

> BA *takes a step forward and collapses on the floor.*

> MA *runs to her, followed by* DAO.

MA: [*to* BA] *Có chuyện dì vậy?* [What's wrong?]

> The HUNGRY GHOST *hovers over her.*

> MA *and* DAO *are at her side.*

> As BA *enacts the possession, the* HUNGRY GHOST *guides her movements as though she is a puppet.*

BA: [*in a lower voice*] There are my girls.

DAO: Why are you talking like that, Ba? You sound like Dad…

BA: You're a good girl. You respect your father. You know how much he suffered.

MA: [*fearfully*] She's possessed…

> DAO *makes a face of disgust and fear. She backs away from* BA.

DAO: Ma, why is she talking like that?

BA: My lovely wife.

MA: [*outraged and afraid*] Don't you lovely me! Why have you come back to haunt us?

BA: I was never gone.

DAO: She's speaking like Dad!

MA: We don't want you here! Leave us now!

BA: I cannot go to the other shore for my sins…

DAO: You don't deserve to go to nirvana! I hate you!

> BA *moves to put a hand on* DAO*'s cheek.* DAO *avoids it.*

Don't you touch me! Don't you dare touch me again!

MA: You leave Dao alone! Leave us alone! The day you left me was the happiest day of my life! We aren't going to honour you anymore…

> BA *turns and stares at* MA.
>
> MA *recoils.*
>
> BA *collapses again.*
>
> *The* HUNGRY GHOST *hovers over her.*
>
> MA *and* DAO *look at each other.*
>
> *Finally* MA *goes to* BA*'s side.*

Dao, call the ambulance…

SCENE FOUR

DAO *comes in to the shrine, eyes red from crying.*

She sees the picture on the shrine and recoils physically.

Then she collapses, shaking, onto the couch.

The HUNGRY GHOST *emerges from the walls.*

DAO: Get away from me! Just get away!

> DAO *shoos the* HUNGRY GHOST *away, in disgust, with her hands.*
>
> *The* HUNGRY GHOST *stops touching her but remains hovering over her.*

Your screams kept me awake at night. Then you would come into my room and… [*She shudders.*] Ma says I'm so lucky being born here, having a roof over my head and enough to eat. But I've been affected by the war too… [*She sits up and cradles herself with her arms. She picks up the conical hat.*] I was just a little girl. I didn't know what was going on. I tried to say I didn't like you. But you're supposed to love and honour your parents… [*She tosses the hat to one side. She starts crying again. Looking up at the picture*] I've been named after your mistress? What was Mum thinking? How would that change anything? Why did she do that to me? What am

I thinking? Does she love me? Or does she hate you more than she loves me? Only Ba loves me and now Ba is... [*She sobs into her hands. She stares directly at the* HUNGRY GHOST.] Why don't we just forget about you? I'm so messed up! One of my male cousin's friends, he was really good to me. He took me everywhere. One night he tried to kiss me and I slapped him. I was so revolted... I could not even hold his hand...

> *Silence.*

I want to be free like my cousins...

> MA *comes into the lounge room.*

> *The* HUNGRY GHOST *watches her.*

> MA *looks at the photo on the shrine and seizes it. In a rage she throws it down onto the floor.*

> *The* HUNGRY GHOST *jerks up and advances towards* MA *menacingly.*

MA: Damn you! Damn you! I curse you to hell!

> *The* HUNGRY GHOST *and* MA *circle each other warily.*

All I sacrificed for you! I gave up working and singing to be a housewife and look after your mother and your daughter for you! But you still left! I've earnt enough merit honouring your memory. I had to pretend you were still with us, better dead than divorced they say. When I heard you died I thought I was free at last... My bad karma. I'm still haunted. [*She looks up at the* HUNGRY GHOST.] Why don't you go away? [*She frowns.*] Dao is all I have. I don't want her to carry on my bad karma... She was a burden at first but now she's everything I'm not—beautiful and free, going to uni... Why didn't I notice? My own daughter? I should have looked after her, not you. She used to cry after you left and I thought it was because she missed you. Now I know better...

> *Her voice breaks.*

> *Silence.*

I don't want Ba to die. Despite it all. I'll do anything to restore her health...

> *She picks up the incense sticks and lights them.*

The HUNGRY GHOST *backs away.*

DAO *stands up and looks at the empty shrine. The photo is still on the floor.*

MA *turns and notices her for the first time.*

Don't pick it up. We're not honouring him anymore.

DAO: You really mean it. No more death ceremonies.

MA: Yes I do. Listen, Dao, there is something I have to tell you. [*Pause.*] What he did to you was unforgivable. I'm not honouring that bastard anymore. Not even for your Ba Noi. [*Pause.*] If I had known what he was doing to you I would have left him and taken you with me.

DAO *begins to cry.*

DAO: I'm so scared. That he might come back and haunt us. I thought he was safely dead. I don't want to sleep tonight. I'll have nightmares like when I was little… We'll be praying for Ba Noi next…

MA *embraces* DAO *and comforts her.*

This family is cursed.

MA: No, Dao. You're not cursed.

Silence.

DAO *looks fearfully at the broken photo frame.*

DAO: Then why did you name me after his mistress? Why did you do that, Mum?

MA *looks down, ashamed.*

MA: I was angry. I was trapped and pregnant when I found out about his mistress. But that doesn't make you cursed, Dao.

Silence.

DAO *looks away, fuming.*

Can you forgive me?

Silence.

MA *looks away. Sighs. She looks at the* áo dài *draped over a chair.* Dao, not all men are like your father.

DAO *snorts.*

No, Dao, listen. There are some gentlemen still out there. There is someone at my work. I want you to meet him…

DAO: Mum, he'll be old! I don't want a boyfriend…

> MA *shakes her head with a smile.*

MA: Not for you, Dao. He's…

> MA *trails off, embarrassed.*

> DAO*'s eyes widen as she realises what* MA *is saying.*

DAO: You have a boyfriend?!

MA: [*shaking her head*] We're just very close. Ssssh. Not now. Ba has to get better. And you can't tell her. I met him after your father left. At work. Your father never wanted me to work outside the house. But once he left us I had to work. I got to know what it was like. What else was out there… But we have to look after Ba now. If she comes back…

DAO: Otherwise she'll be a hungry ghost like Dad…

> DAO *starts shaking.*

MA: Ba would not be a hungry ghost. She has nothing to be ashamed of. [*Stronger*] Will you forgive me, Dao? If we are angry at each other we cannot exorcise your father… I've been bitter enough. Can you?

> DAO *looks* MA *in the face, then relents.*

DAO: I know you love me, Mum.

MA: I do, Dao. And we'll exorcise him tomorrow. Together.

> *She hands an incense stick to* DAO *who bows to the altar.*

> *The* HUNGRY GHOST *begins to retreat from* DAO *and* MA *and heads towards* BA.

SCENE FIVE

BA *is moving freely in front of the stage. Her hair is down and she is dressed in white.*

Ghost music plays.

The HUNGRY GHOST *dances around her.*

BA *stares into the audience.*

BA: You see what you see. I see what I see. Alone in this room I speak with the living and the dead.

> *A bell sounds.*

Audible whispering from HUNGRY GHOSTS.

HUNGRY GHOSTS: [*in a mixture of Vietnamese and English*] *Cho ăn đi. Cúng đi. Làm quỉ đói đi.* [Feed us. Honour us. Become one of us.] [*repeated*]

> BA *goes over to the shrine and stares at the picture of her son thrown to the ground.*

BA: I know now. I know you now.

HUNGRY GHOSTS: You know, you know.

BA: I know that you are not what I thought you are.

> *The* HUNGRY GHOST *comes towards her.*

I don't believe what you did to Dao. She was just a little girl. How could you? [*She scratches her rashes. She holds her head in her hands.*] You are not my son. How can you be my son to do such a thing? [*Whispering*] I'm so ashamed of my son. When you left me in your wife's care I should have let you go. The truth was I could not look you in the eye anymore. I'm so ashamed. Because I abandoned you in that orphanage. And that's what turned you bad. When I took you back you wagged school. You refused to wear shoes and you wouldn't listen to me. Then the war came. When you came back to us at first I was so happy. But then I realised you had turned distant and cold. I thought once you got married and had little Dao things would get better. Oh, my son. History wrecked your chances at happiness. You were my child until the war gave me back a stranger.

> *The* HUNGRY GHOST *circle* BA.

HUNGRY GHOSTS: You bear the family's shame. Join us. Come and join us.

BA: It would be so easy now to give up and go to sleep.

> *Silence.*

> *A bell sounds.*

> DAO *and* MA*'s voices are heard praying. With each verse the* HUNGRY GHOST *retreats from* BA. *(These next two verses are spoken simultaneously.)*

MA:
As if a fire is raging on all four sides,

A hungry ghost ceaselessly suffers from heat
Hungry ghost now to be born in a Pure Land
Hear this gatha transmitted by the Buddha
Hungry ghosts have acted unskillfully

DAO:

With craving, hatred and ignorance
Manifested in actions of body, speech and mind.
All hungry ghosts repent of this.

Bell.

O hungry ghosts

MA & DAO: [*together*]

We make offerings of food
Multiplied in the ten directions
So that you can all receive them
By the merit of this offering
May we and all hungry ghosts
Be successful in the realisation of the path.

Bell.

HUNGRY GHOSTS: Acknowledging our suffering, we see the root of our suffering. Touching the root of our suffering, our suffering ceases.

The HUNGRY GHOST *lets go of* BA *and disappears.*

BA *looks after it longingly before returning to her hospital bed and closing her eyes.*

SCENE SIX

BA *is in her hospital bed, her eyes closed.*

DAO *and* MA *sit on either side of her.*

DAO: I didn't know she was so far gone. If I had known…
MA: I tried to tell you.
DAO: I know.

Silence.

MA: I don't want you to bear my bad karma, Dao. I want you to find a nice boy who won't betray you.

DAO *begins to cry.*

DAO: I know you want the best for me, Mum. So does Ba. If she wakes up I promise I'll be home more and keep her company. Then you can go out more with your boyfriend...

They embrace.

BA*'s eyes open. She is groggy and unaware of where she is.*

BA: *Tôi đang ở đâu đây?* [Where am I?]

A bell sounds.

She looks around and sees only MA *and* DAO.

MA: *Má đang ở bịnh viện. Má bị xỉu.* [In the hospital again, Ba. You collapsed.]

BA: My son. He's gone. Hasn't he?

DAO *and* MA *look at each other.*

MA *looks searchingly at* BA*'s face.*

MA: Yes, I think he has.

SCENE SEVEN

BA *sits at home by herself, staring at the place where her son's picture used to be. She is wearing her new slippers.*

BA: I see what I see... [*She looks around for the* HUNGRY GHOSTS. *She sees nothing.*] We have banished them forever. [*She hums to herself the melody of the love song that* MA *sang earlier. Directly to the audience*] This boyfriend cannot replace my son. [*Pause.*] He cannot treat me as badly as I've been treated by my eldest son.

BA *breathes in and out.*

MA, *wearing the* áo dài, *and* DAO *come on stage.*

BA *looks up expecting to see the* HUNGRY GHOSTS. *She relaxes when she sees who it is.*

DAO: What are you doing up? You should be in bed, Ba.

BA *looks at her family kindly.*

BA: There is nothing to be afraid of anymore.

DAO: Really?

MA: Really. The doctor says you're very lucky. You have to be more careful, you almost...

BA: [*interrupting*] I am very lucky. To have you and Dao praying for my good health. [*She looks at* MA *side-on, and smiles to herself.*] So when are you bring this boyfriend to meet me?

> MA *is stunned.*

MA: I…

BA: Wait till I am stronger and I can cook for you. Then maybe we can all go back to Vietnam together and visit Auntie Chi…

> MA *and* DAO *laugh with joy.*
>
> *A bell sounds.*

THE END

 **presents**

SILENCE
A Hungry Ghosts Production

Written by
Hoa Pham

Dramaturgy
Kit Lazaroo

Directed by
Wolf Heidecker

Director of Puppetry
Penelope Bartlau

Sound Designer
Simon Charles

Stage Manager/ Sound/Lx-Operators
Amber Hart, Canada White

Lx Designer
Rebecca Etchell

Set Designer
Lisa Hoebartner

Actors:
Ba (the grandmother)
Gabrielle Chan

Ma (the mother)
Diana Nguyen

Dao (the daughter)
Ai Diem Le

Puppeteer
Bronwen Kamasz

Puppeteer (and movement advisor)
Paul Bongiorno

Cover Artwork by Nedd Jones. Photo by Ross Calsa at stripesphotography.com

Hungry Ghosts Productions wishes to thank the following organizations and individuals for their wonderful support: Richmond Uniting Church; Huu Tran; Kai Raisbeck; Tony Albers/Doodleism; Michael Cosgriff; David Sivaraj; Sohrab Partow; Carl Preusker, Jeff Kaufman, Jo Moulday; Rob Lingham; Benita Dass-Grässe; Doan Kim Van; James Adler/Eagle's Nest Theatre; La Mama management and staff.

This project is supported by VicHealth as part of its program to promote diversity and reduce race-based discrimination.

LA MAMA

Artistic Director
Liz Jones
Company Manager
Pippa Bainbridge
Publicist/Education officer
Maureen Hartley
Marketing Coordinator
Louise Jones
Communications Coordinator
Nedd Jones
House Managers
Lisa Hoebartner & Rebecca Etchell
Community Outreach
Mary Helen Sassman & Caitlin Dullard

COMMITTEE OF MANAGEMENT:
Edwin Batt, Liz Jones, Duré Dara, Mark Rubbo, Tim Stitz, Caroline Lee, Rhonda Day and Emily Harms.

FRONT OF HOUSE STAFF:
The regular staff and: Liz McColl, Jenny Andersen, Jo-Anne Armstrong, Bree Hartley, Alicia Benn-Lawler, Mari Lourey, Laurence Strangio, Phil Roberts, Debra Low, Nicola Gunn, Talya Chalef, Merrilee Moss, Laura Hegyesi, Ray Triggs, Nic Velissaris and Christy Flaws.

La Mama's Committee of Management, Staff and its wider theatrical community acknowledge that our theatre is on traditional Wurundjeri land. La Mama is financially assisted by the Australian Government through the Australia Council – its Arts Funding and Advisory body – and the Victorian Government through Arts Victoria – Department of Premier and Cabinet, and the Community Support Fund. La Mama productions are financially supported by the City of Melbourne. Our thanks to the Management and staff of Readings Bookshop, Carlton, for their contribution to the running of the Box Office.

PRODUCTION NOTES FOR
SILENCE 2009-2010

Authors notes for *Silence:* Hoa Pham

I wanted to write a play to break down the silence in Vietnamese-Australian women's lives. There is a cultural taboo against telling outsiders about family issues and problems which means that many women's voices are not heard. To this end I interviewed six women aged between 25 and 65 about their life experiences. I distilled their stories into play form with the help of Gorkem Acaroglu, Tony Le Nguyen, Australian Vietnamese Women's Association, Angela Costi, Melanie Beddie, Ai Diem Le, HaiHa Le and Mong Diep. I have been fortunate enough to have the support of La Mama Theatre from the play's inception and of Melbourne City Council during the first years of the process. The 2009–10 production owes its form to Kit Lazaroo, Penelope Bartlau and Wolf Heidecker. Their visions for the play have made it what it is today. The 2009–10 production was selected to be a part of La Mama's VicHealth funded work which uses the arts to promote cultural diversity. I hope that **Silence** shares some of the suffering and stories of survival of Vietnamese-Australian women with a broad audience, and raises awareness of some poignant issues within many communities.

Dramaturgical notes for *Silence:* Kit Lazaroo

Silence is a play about a family of Australian-Vietnamese women who are imprisoned by the past because of their habits of silence. They represent three generations, each with different experiences of both Vietnam and Australia. They are due to honour the father on the anniversary of his death, but there is so much that is unspoken about what he really means to each of them in different ways, that they are unable to proceed with the ceremony in a harmonious manner until they find a way out of the silence. As well as being a play about the past and the longevity of trauma, it is a play about the conflict between desire and tradition.

Style

The play is written in a mostly realistic style. A number of conversations are interspersed with the characters thinking out loud. The strength of the realism and the domestic setting is that it suggests that the ghosts are real presences, rather than a metaphor for memory or the past. This makes them potentially more malignant.

Setting and Worlds

While the setting is very domestic and interior, there is the sense that it co-exists with other worlds. For instance, the material world is infused with a spiritual world, and beyond the walls of the house there is a different Australia (represented by Stacey) and Vietnam (Auntie Chi) where there is greater freedom from the past than within the walls of the house. Interestingly, Vietnam exists within the house as well, but here it is the old and frightening Vietnam of Ba's memories, a place where hospitals buy the blood of desperate women.

Characters

The three women direct their energy towards different spheres. Ba directs much of her energy inwardly and towards the past; Ma directs hers mostly at the business of the present moment (sorting the greens); Dao, I think, is directing her energy at battering down the walls of her prison—her energy is more volatile and restless in its movements. However, each of them suffers a similar conflict between their sense of duty and their true feelings, or desire for freedom. This conflict surfaces as complaints and bickering, but underneath that is a strong undercurrent of love for each other.

Ghosts/Father

The ghosts keep altering their manifestations, starting fairly innocuously as cats and becoming increasingly invasive. They are not inside Ba's head, but are real, clamouring for attention, not yet noticed by the younger women. Although frightening, they are also objects of our pity because they are damaged through violence and conflict.

It is interesting that while the Father is the subject that the women keep silent about, in this draft it is his action in invading Ba's body to draw attention to himself and to reconnect with his daughter, that finally forces the end to the silence, something that was hard for the women to achieve by themselves. This gives the ghost a more powerful dramatic purpose. Because the silence is broken, the women are able to draw together to give the ghost peace, so completing the cycle of restlessness and need.

Silence

There are different kinds of silence. There is the silence of avoidance, and the silence that occurs when people are talking at cross purposes to each other. There is also the silence of deep thought, and the silence of shock, trauma, being numb. There is the silence of waiting to see what has happened, the silence of oblivion, and then peace.

War and Trauma

The war in Vietnam is still going on inside Ba's head, and it lives on in all three women and the ghost too, in different ways. It is as though the historical, political war has given birth to other personal wars in the bodies and minds of every generation. The Father's abuse of Dao is a symptom of the brutalisation of war and the way personal neediness becomes monstrous and damaging when one is finally overwhelmed. The mother Ma in comparison, although at times also selfish, needy and hurtful, has been lucky to remain grounded through love. The Buddhist chants and precepts counterbalance the monstrous damage, so that again the women complete a cycle, moving away from honouring tradition, but also returning to it at a deeper level.

Puppetry Director's notes for *Silence:* Penelope Bartlau

Silence is a dream script for a puppetry director. Hidden within the naturalism are deep layers and textures that can be explored and expressed visually. The ghosts will be created through the employment of some of the techniques of Bunraku puppetry, a traditional Japanese form of puppet theatre wherein multiple puppeteers operate the puppet. Additionally we will use rod puppet techniques and mask. We have two puppeteers working on the production to manipulate the terrifying spectre of the man who will not leave the family alone. The puppet will appear from multiple locations within the set (we will have a total of at least eight different versions of the character hidden amongst the set). The puppet/spectre will be invisible—at times it will be part of the furniture and will manifest from and retreat into these hiding places. To see a house in a dream, it is a representation of the soul and the self. The ghost in the house in *Silence* is a metaphor for the unresolved issues of each of character in the play: the grief, confusion, love and anger about the man who was a father, a husband and a son in this household.

The aim of the artistic direction and the puppetry is not to impose on the drama as it unfolds, but rather to strengthen and enrich it. We have chosen simple designs, based on Vietnamese hungry ghosts, to make the play otherworldly, beautiful and compelling.

Director's notes for *Silence*: Wolf Heidecker

Three women, three generations, three life experiences; interlinked fates, interdependent relationships, intricate and revealing stories. *Silence* is full of humaneness (as distinct from *humanity*), full of common behaviour to be found where people are in search for happiness despite all the trauma experienced, despite the secrets and denial maintained as a seemingly 'easy way out'. Resilience through love and care.

Though enveloped in Vietnamese culture, *Silence* is not just an 'ethnic' play. Yet, the centrepiece of the set design strongly refers to Vietnamese culture (i.e. ancestor worship). Central to the stage is the Family Shrine, dominant and colourful, very much in contrast to the plain colours of the soft, waving walls and the predominantly cubic structures used as furniture. The attentive observer will also find some behavioural details that comment on cultural differences in the physical interaction between the characters.

Though told from a female point of view, **Silence** is not just a 'feminist' statement. And yet the stories of the three women are more or less about the impact the most important man in their respective lives had and still has, the late son, husband and father whose eerie presence is still felt.

Though referring to Buddhist philosophy, **Silence** is not just about a belief system. Yet, there are a number of references to Buddhist rites and citations. There are also situations where superstition, deeply inherent in Vietnamese culture, becomes prevalent.

Silence is about secrets, about denial, about covering up. The set design takes that into account by placing the action in a room made of waving fabric, rather than solid walls. The sparse pieces of furniture are just functional, not commenting on the economic status of the family. There is also plain fabric loosely draped over most of the furniture, covering, hiding. The puppets are single-coloured too, white/off white. White in Vietnamese culture represents Death.

Primarily, the lighting design highlights the dramatic development of the story-telling and suggests diverse atmospheres in a way that gives the audience space to intensify their respective feelings, using their own imagination. Most of the overall atmosphere creation is done using the sound-scape which is also a vital component of this production.

Life is suffering. Identifying the root of suffering, then touching the root of suffering, one ceases to suffer.

—The Four Noble Truths, Buddhism

HOA PHAM
AUTHOR

ACKNOWLEDGEMENTS

Hoa Pham is an author and psychologist. She has published four books (including *Quicksilver* and *Vixen*) and a number of short stories. Two of her three plays (*49 Ghosts* and *I Could Be You*) have been produced. Hoa was the President of Australian Vietnamese Youth Media for the last three years, and has started her own production company, Hungry Ghosts. She participated in the Go Show as part of the 2008 Melbourne International Festival. She recently returned from an International Writers' Exchange in Berlin.

For more information on Hoa Pham, visit: www.hoapham.net. Hoa is also the founding editor of *Peril*—an Asian-Australian arts and culture magazine: www.peril.com.au

Silence was initially conceived in 2007. I wished to address the issue of women's silence in the Vietnamese-Australian community and interviewed six women aged from 25–65 in 2007. I was deeply moved by their stories and undertook to write the play drawing on elements of each of their life experiences. I'd like to thank these women for their generosity and sharing personal experiences with me. This play is dedicated to both my grandmothers for their wisdom and their stories.
Hoa Pham/Playwright

KIT LAZAROO
DRAMATURG

WOLF HEIDECKER
DIRECTOR

Kit Lazaroo is a playwright whose work includes: *Hospital of the Lost Coin / The Vanishing Box* (La Mama, 2003) which was nominated for a Green Room Award for writing; *True Adventures of a Soul Lost at Sea*, a recipient of an RE Ross Trust Playwright's Award, *Asylum*, nominated for a Green Room Award and the 2006 Wal Cherry Play of the Year. *Asylum* enjoyed a sell-out season at La Mama in March 2007 and was shortlisted for the Queensland and Victorian Premiers' Literary Awards. Kit has also written *Letters from Animals*, shortlisted for the Max Afford Memorial Prize 2004 and produced in 2007. *Topsy* received an RE Ross Playwright's Award in 2007 and is due for production at fortyfive downstairs in 2010. Kit is also an inner city GP and has recently completed a PhD looking at creative approaches to fostering a 'community of memory' among older Chinese East Timorese refugees.

Wolf Heidecker came to Australia in 1997 with more than 25 years of experience as artistic director, Theatre-Admin/PR-officer, Tour Manager, and CEO/General Manager with several German opera and theatre companies. In Australia he has worked with the Queensland Philharmonic Orchestra, the Flying Fruit Fly Circus and Wyndham Cultural Centre. Wolf is a trained performing artist/director, Business Economist, Psychotherapist and Civil Celebrant. Today he manages his Arts/Business and Management Consultancy and directs and produces with Larrikin Ensemble Theatre, TopArtProductions and Many Moons Group Inc in Melbourne. His most recent productions include *Haneef: The Interrogation* by Graham Pitts, *Trio* by Dina Ross, and *Silence* by Hoa Pham (all for La Mama), *Cymbeline* by W. Shakespeare and *The Trial Of God* by Elie Wiesel.

PENELOPE BARTLAU
DIRECTOR OF PUPPETRY

Penelope Bartlau is Artistic Director of Barking Spider Visual Theatre, and is a theatre maker, writer, director, dramaturg and puppeteer. She has been working professionally for over twenty years. Her qualifications include a Master of Puppetry, Victorian College of the Arts (2007); Professional Screenwriting, RMIT (01); Commedia Dell'Arte, Antonio Fava, Italy; Lee Strasberg Institute, New York City; New York University, *20th Century American Fine Art and Design*, (with Harold Jaffy) (95-96); Bachelor of Arts, Monash University, Politics and English Literature Majors (1989).

GABRIELLE CHAN
ACTOR – BA

Gabrielle Chan is an actress who specialises in Chinese Opera as well as film and TV. Her recent credits include *Home Song Stories, The Last Chip, Celestial Avenue* and episodes of *City Homicide* for television.

This is her first production for La Mama.

DIANA NGUYEN
ACTOR - MA

Diana Nguyen is reprising the role of Ma for this new production of *Silence*. She is currently rehearsing for the Big West Festival for *Generation/Translations* production. She performed *Miss Saigon* (CLOC), 2008 Melbourne Comedy Festival (Dantes), 2007 Melbourne Short and Sweet Festival and 2008 Short but not Sweet Festival where she was nominated for Best Actress in *Death by 1000 Cuts* and *The People Upstairs*. Diana's writing credits include *Like Tears in the Rain,* a play about her mother's Vietnamese refugee experience for the 2008 Melbourne Fringe and Alice Pung's short story collection *Five ways to disappoint your Vietnamese mother*. Her other acting credits include *Fat Camp* (Sisters Grimm), *King Turd* (PipeDream), feature and short film productions and Educational school performances for BooBook Theatre. Diana also performed in *Generation/Translations* (Big West Festival 2009).

AI DIEM LE
ACTOR - DAO

Ai Diem Le: Passionate artisan, works as hard as she can, is a humanist, situationalist, not into working for the man. Singing is her everything, everything is her drama, drama in stage, life conferred she can't be caged. So she draws and paints, is sharing, very caring, completely over bearing, delirious and sensually curious. Lately heart bruised, youth used, creatively mental and is still in a rental. Her cooking is funky she hoards and own all things junky. She moves like a gypsy you'll rarely find her tipsy unless crooning and misty, spooning and frisky in love, for love why love, it's all about love. To be further exposed beyond this prose and how she keeps on her toes, regards from aidiem.com

PAUL BONGIORNO
PUPPETEER AND MOVEMENT ADVISOR

SIMON CHARLES
SOUND DESIGNER

Paul Bongiorno is a Melbourne-based physical theatre actor. He started life as a martial artist and competitive freestyle wrestler. He then thought it better to use his people throwing skills for good rather than evil. His unorthodox performance development path led him through gymnastics and acrobatics, circus, theatre, musicals and surprisingly even serious roles for film and television. He performed in *Kids can get Lost* in the Next Wave Festival, Fregmonto Stoke's operatic master opus *The Endarkenment*, and cheerfully chucked cheering cheerleaders meters in the air for the cheer national titles. He has acted in numerous short films, been in *Rush* and *City Homicide*, and the odd re-enactment for SBS or ABC docos. He regularly performs acrobatic and dance gigs.

As a composer, **Simon Charles** has been the recipient of several prizes, including Zavod Jazz/Classical Fusion Award and the Marion Isabel Thomas Prize. His works have been performed in Australia, Thailand and Sweden. He has been invited to the Asian Composer's League festival and conference for new music in Bangkok as a young Australian delegate. He has also been Artist in Residence in the writer's cottage at Bundanon, a property donated by Arthur Boyd in NSW. Simon is currently undertaking a Master of Music Performance degree at the VCA. During this study, he has developed his practice as an improvising musician, and has composed and conducted several new works for chamber ensemble. Simon has worked as a composer and sound designer on various performance projects, including the dance work *Pay No Attention to the Man Behind the Curtain* by Alisdair MacIndoe performed at the Next Wave festival, and *Marionette* by poet Jess Wilkinson, performed at the This is Not Art Festival in Newcastle.

CANADA WHITE
STAGE MANAGER/SOUND/LX OPERATOR

After completing a Bachelor of Economics and a Diploma of Live Production – Theatre and Events, **Canada White** has worked as a production manager, stage manager, technical manager / operator and arts administrator for numerous established and up-and-coming arts companies including: TopArtPartners, Verve Studios, The Victorian College of the Arts (Drama School), Auspicious Arts Projects Inc., Latrobe University, Louise Withers and Associates, Theatre@Risk, Event Logistics, Optic Nerve Performance Group, The Hayloft Project, Eaglesnest Theatre, Theatre Works and La Mama.

AMBER HART
STAGE MANAGER/SOUND/LX OPERATOR

Amber Hart first took acting classes at age 7 with Bryan Brown. Inspired, she went on to graduate a Bachelor of Theatre at UWS. In 2002 Amber joined Wincap Productions to make the feature film *Picture This*, and later joined Pepperkorn Productions, writing material and touring popular Sydney venues. In Melbourne, Amber has stage managed *The Trial of God* with Eaglesnest Theatre, Stage managed *Trio*, under Larrikin Ensemble, and designed the lighting and operated lights and sound for Many Moons Productions *Fusion DownUnder*, and *Bengal Live*.

BRONWEN KAMASZ
PUPPETEER

Bronwen Kamasz trained as a sculptor in Perth. Her artistic practice then developed into Installation and performance art. Along side her Fine Arts degree Bronwen had a passion for puppets and puppetry that stemmed from seeing Phillipe Genty Company perform, as a child.

In 2009 Bronwen re-located to Melbourne to experience the outstanding Puppetry course at the VCA (now sadly not running). This year is a focus of performer training including Suzuki method and clown. Bronwen is honoured to be a part of the story of *Silence*.

REBECCA ETCHELL
LIGHTING DESIGNER

Rebecca Etchell is a Melbourne based lighting designer, set designer, stage manager and production manager and has worked for many theatres and theatre companies both at home and abroad. She has spent the last 6 years as a tour manager and set designer for British comedian Ross Noble. During this time she has managed to squeeze in some design work for The Dream Festival, a NAB sponsored event where she was commissioned to design a large format, illuminated inflatable sculpture which was exhibited on the banks of the Yarra River.

She also recently designed for Theatre Works' production of *At The Sans Hotel*, which was an adaptation of the original La Mama production *My Friend Schadenfreude* (2009).

She is currently employed with La Mama as the House Manager.

LISA HOEBARTNER
SET DESIGNER

Lisa Hoebartner studied Graphic Design in Portugal, and, in 2008, graduated with a Master of Arts, Set and Film Design, from the University of Applied Arts (Vienna, Austria). Previously Lisa had been a Pedagogical Program Developer, a Tour Guide, a Teacher of Art and Painting, and worked in a film production office.

In 2002 she was assistant Set and Costume Designer for *Macbeth*, directed by Barrie Kosky (Schauspielhaus, Vienna). Since coming to Melbourne Lisa has worked as a Barista and been a Volunteer for The Wilderness Society. She is currently one of La Mama's House Managers, and continues to pursue her interest in Set Design for Theatre.

STANDING OVATION FOR
STATE'S SMALLEST THEATRE

In 2010, La Mama will celebrate 43 years of nurturing new Australian Theatre.

Built in 1883 for Anthony Reuben Ford, a Carlton printer, the building in Faraday Street had been used as a workshop, a boot and shoe factory, an electrical engineering workshop and a silk underwear factory before becoming a theatre in 1967. It was established by Betty Burstall and modelled on experimental theatre activities in New York. Jack Hibberd's play Three Old Friends was the first play performed in the tiny space. Since that time the crowded intimacy of La Mama has provided welcome opportunities to a host of playwrights, actors, directors, technicians, film-makers, poets and comedians, such as David Williamson, Barry Dickins, John Romeril, Tes Lyssiotis, Lloyd Jones, the Cantrills, Judith Lucy, Richard Frankland, Julia Zemiro, and Cate Blanchett... the list of those who have been nurtured there is long.

In 1975 Barry Oakley described La Mama as 'a village phenomenon, a Carlton phenomenon'. Now, in 2010, under the capable care of Liz Jones (Artistic Director since 1976), and her La Mama team, approximately 50 productions are produced annually (at La Mama, and the Carlton Courthouse in Drummond Street) and an ever-increasing audience is drawn not only from the Carlton and Melbourne University environs, but from far and wide across the country.

'I set La Mama up, as a space for writers and directors to perform in but also it was a space where people came, as audience, to participate in the creative experiment.'
—Betty Burstall, 1987, Artistic Director of La Mama 1967-76

'Much will be said of La Mama's role in developing a new generation of Australian writing. However, in considering policies and personalities, one should not forget the nature of the space and its impact in making possible performances that would be lost in a large theatre. It gave performances the intimacy of the cinema close-up with the exciting immediacy of the live theatre and the warmth of the coffee lounge.'

—Daryl Wilkinson, 1986, Director
From La Mama... the story of a theatre

La Mama Theatre – which, on various occasions, has been called headquarters, the source, the shopfront and the birthplace of Australian theatre – was classified by the National Trust in 1999.

'The two story brick building is of State cultural significance because it has been occupied by La Mama Theatre... The building is indelibly associated with the performance arts and is a rare manifestation of an experimental theatre in Australia...'
—National Trust Classification Report

When it comes to grassroots Melbourne theatre, La Mama in Carlton is like the 60GB iPod – small, subtle, but containing a whole lot more than you might expect.
—John Bailey, The Age. E.G. 29/06/05

La Mama produces work at both venues: 205 Faraday Street, Carlton, and at the La Mama Courthouse, 349 Drummond Street, Carlton.

www.currency.com.au

Visit Currency Press' new website now:

- Buy your books online
- Browse through our full list of titles, from plays to screenplays, books on theatre, film and music, and more
- Choose a play for your school or amateur performance group by cast size and gender
- Obtain information about performance rights
- Find out about theatre productions and other performing arts news across Australia
- For students, read our study guides
- For teachers, access syllabus and other relevant information
- Sign up for our email newsletter

The performing arts publisher